LIVING WILL

Living Will

POEMS BY DAVID HILTON

COFFEE HOUSE PRESS
Minneapolis

COPYRIGHT © 2007 Joanne Hilton
COVER PHOTOGRAPH © Getty Images
AUTHOR PHOTOGRAPH © Susan Laferla
COVER & BOOK DESIGN Linda S. Koutsky

Coffee House Press books are available to the trade through our primary distributor, Consortium Book Sales & Distribution, 1045 Westgate Drive, Saint Paul, MN 55114. For personal orders, catalogs, or other information, write to: Coffee House Press, 27 North Fourth Street, Suite 400, Minneapolis, MN 55401.

Coffee House Press is a nonprofit literary publishing house. Support from private foundations, corporate giving programs, government programs, and generous individuals helps make the publication of our books possible. We gratefully acknowledge their support in detail in the back of this book.

Library of Congress Cataloging-in-Publication Data
Hilton, David, 1938–2005.
Living will : poems / by David Hilton.
p. cm.
ISBN-13: 978-1-56689-200-1 (alk. paper)
ISBN-10: 1-56689-200-7 (alk. paper)
I. Title.
PS3558.I47L58 2007
811'.54—DC22
2006039208

FIRST EDITION | FIRST PRINTING
1 3 5 7 9 8 6 4 2
Printed in the United States

Poems in this book have appeared in the following publications: "Crofter Tea, Skye," *Beloit Poetry Journal;* "Drinking Buddy," *Baltimore Sunday Sun Magazine* and *Beloit Poetry Journal;* "The Grownup," *Yale Review;* "Halloween: An Oncology," *Beloit Poetry Journal;* "La Familia Sagrada," *Poet Lore;* "Living Will," *Talking River Review;* "Lost Nest," *Defined Providence;* "The Man with No Face," *Poetry Northwest;* "Mass at Rathmullen," *Beloit Poetry Journal;* "Nights of '67: For Darrell Gray," *Exquisite Corpse;* "Old Drafts," *Poetry Northwest;* "Old Poet," *Poet Lore;* "Remembering Aunt Tilly," *5AM;* "Salcombe Ramble," *Yale Review;* "November Burial" and "Summer, Berkeley, 1969," *Long Shot;* "Tin Whistle," *Poetry Northwest;* "To Find the Standing Stones at Kenmare, Go . . ." *Beloit Poetry Journal.*

for Joanne, much-named beneficiary
of my everlasting love, whose heart feels—
for all the world—inextricable from mine.
Let's both cry *"god-damn,"* my dearest . . .

Contents

Foreword

I met David Hilton in 1968, at a poetry reading at the University of Wisconsin–Madison. I was twenty-four and about to have my first collection of poetry published by a local small press. David was thirty and had a group of poems in an anthology, *Quickly Aging Here,* published by Anchor. It would have been easy for me to be jealous of this interloper, who was an English grad student, while I was pursuing a decidedly nonliterary degree in chemistry.

But we soon discovered that we wrote in different styles, and about different subject matter. We both liked telling stories about "real gardens with real toads" as David once described his literary goals. So we decided to be friends instead, and started a relationship driven by our writing that lasted thirty-seven years.

David married Joanne in the early seventies, and that relationship lasted until his death as well. They were childless, but didn't seem to mind. They both were dedicated teachers and travelers. David's poems were his children, and he took the responsibility of rearing them very seriously. Although he published three full-length collections, a number of chapbooks, and was regularly anthologized, he was remarkably resistant to what we called "poetry business," including the grantsmanship and self-promotion often essential to becoming a "name poet." Although he admired the work of many of his forebears: Galway Kinnell, Theodore Roethke, W. S. Merwin, William Stafford, and Gary Snyder to name a few, he was not a workshop "product," and he never had a living mentor. He always saw his association with the Actualist Movement, managed by Morty Sklar, Dave Mattingly, and other writers in the Iowa City area, as a great goof, and I think that most of the other "members" did so as well.

Although it is an overused term, David would have been proud to have been called a "poet's poet." I think he is the best mature poet I know of who is not yet well-known, although he wrote and published continuously until his too-early death in

9

2005 at the age of sixty-seven. I hope this collection will bring him the wider audience he always deserved.

Poets worry about dry spells, but early in the seventies, David said, with confidence, that he was not worried about being able to write his next poem, and he was right. Early on, we agreed to be each other's harshest critic, but also agreed that we would not take offense at the criticism that we received from each other, no matter how disappointing. We kept exchanging draft poems until shortly before his death; it was a rare and irreplaceable partnership.

Although, for his entire career, he taught at a community college and was not an editor or regular reviewer, David attracted the friendship and support of many better-known writers and editors, who shared only their dedication to writing and their individuality: Andrei Codrescu, Michael Lally, Anselm Hollo, David Clewell, Joe Cardarelli, Terry Winch, Darrell Gray, Morty Sklar, Michael Andre, and Allan Kornblum, to name just a few.

David was fearless as a writer. He would write about anything, including his abused mother and his hopeless childhood, his drinking (which he abandoned years ago), nursing his wife after a nearly fatal car accident, his sex life or his cancer; no subject was out of bounds. He could write comfortably in every modern style. David preferred to write long poems with long lines, and his poems lengthened as he matured as a writer. He had an ear for the voices of the down-and-out and the eccentric that was unflinchingly honest. He didn't just catalog them, he embraced them, and investigated their reasons for being with respect and humor. Poems like "The Man with No Face" and "Remembering Aunt Tilly" don't just suggest Arbus photos she could have taken; they illuminate her work.

Likewise, the poems that came out of David's trips to Mexico and Europe reach far beyond the literary postcards that poets typically produce on their sabbaticals. Particularly in his poems about Ireland, he casts long, sinewy lines to draw in ancient runes and ruins, teahouses, masses, and sheep. At once specific and mythic, poems like "Salcombe Ramble" and "To Find the Standing Stones at Kenmare, Go" open like a guidebook you might find in a dream about an ancient lending library run by druids.

A few years ago, he decided to try rhyme. Suddenly all his poems rhymed! He did it so well that I didn't notice it for a year. Another time, we decided to try writing prose poems about single pop songs. I had in mind a free-form paragraph or two of hip impressions. David wrote a stunning six-page poem about one obscure R&B instrumental by Chuck Higgins and a four-page poem about a Big Joe Turner hit, and never wrote another. Inspired by Richard Hugo, we decided to try "letter poems." David wrote exactly one, and it opens this collection.

In the last months of David's life, I tried to keep a poetic conversation going by suggesting that we exchange short postcard-sized poems. We only exchanged a few, but one sums up David's passion for life and for poetry very well:

1970

Woke in the dark on my back,
nailed to the floor by my two-
gallon Mountain Red hangover—
& mescaline, sweet opium hash.
What day was that? Was this?
Rain through a wide open window.
I can twitch my toes. Yes, OK!
Someone's taking a long sleepy piss.
Already poetry is reviving,
no matter the damage. Friends
soon will regather—
the room again a roaring
blast furnace of poems.

—Warren Woessner
Minneapolis, September 2006

Letter to Woessner from Glen Burnie

Dear Warren: A new apartment furnished with the death rattles
of crickets on an early fall evening. Already I'm known
by name at Drug Fair; the varicose waitress calls me
"Tuna on Toast with Tomato," which she cannot know
is a "metre-making argument" natural child-warbler
of the spermy winds that she is.
One of my colleagues mourned to me yesterday
that she's "struggling through imagery."
Today is Thursday night, which I've decided
to live as if Friday didn't count—I'll see
how far back I can push the week—maybe
get wrecked beginning on the Sabbath.

I shall declare for Stevens at last,
as we all shall if a drop of poet is within us:
"Not ideas about the thing, but the thing itself."
Drive it all back to the tan spider now launching
a strand down from my burning candle.
I can hear the freeway from here—a rustle
so natural that I think of green, cool tires.
A mile away there's a barn collapsed
up to its roof, set in the field
like an inverted ark, an offering.
Every now and then, sometimes
not for days, a car will slow down
and someone will point to the warm, brown ruin.
It's that person I want to know.
Love, Dave.

Summer, Berkeley, 1969

Crystal fired the burnt
umber hillside—everyone tripping
to chords and quarks on KSAN
crunching and throbbing the
long breath of the universe we
danced within—and there, exposed
to all eyes flowing through
cobalt, ruby, emerald, purple shades,
vibrating on the golden grass
sloping up from the moist creekside trail,
in the chance sunlit circle
allowed by looming eucalyptus,
the boy and girl fucked slowly,
luxuriating, his torso
tensile upward, head back,
her legs spread wide,
rising, like wings.
One rhythm at the center—
they might have composed an asana
but for their riding-rocking easy
quickening and the boy's long
blond hair whipping
and the girl's feet trembling.
And they were silent,
their gasps and cries
inseparable from the sun's pulsing,
or carried away by
Strawberry Canyon's six-inch
waterfalls and birds' barking.

And no one hooted or laughed,
but gestured *quiet* to those behind,
pointed, smiled—green-shadowed
beneath those great pungent leaves,
in the fleeting forever of it—
then, lingeringly, moved on.
That was this instant, that was
this now: glistening, burnished
heat of 1969, the woman
embraced by the soft-bearded earth,
embracing and holding,
enfolding the levitating boy,
and all our poetry aspiring
to the condition of such fucking.

Nights of '67: For Darrell Gray

It is enough to have wanted to be John Keats
debating Gaston Bachelard in a one-room room—
oh, we all lived in "rooms"—book-crowded mattress
on floor, "stereo" speakers exquisitely placed,
table bare but for typewriter and debris,
and great jugs of Carlo Rossi's mountain red
amid strewn "albums," same four or five
played all night. Remember?—Miles, *Aftermath,*
Sgt. Pepper, Quicksilver's *Happy Trails,*
always some Beach Boys, Country Joe,
Dylan, Janis, Airplane . . . and always a "lid"
($15–$20) spread on a sheet
of typing paper (with a poem lost on it),
winnowed of seeds & stems, clean weed mounded
into huge "bombers" we chainsmoked in those days
of mild Mexican grass (pre-sens), missed seeds
popping out and burning tell-tale holes
in our T-shirts—

when there was no politics
but righteous causes, and excitement like what
a Deep Image is, what metaphor *does,*
and Neruda, Garuda, Dada, Baba Ram Das,
legends of acid, reading all of "Asphodel"
perfectly one thrilling 3 A.M and I knew
all I needed then, Darrell's voice so young—
my 22-year-old mentor—husky-pure
from unfiltered Camels (that never got to kill him)
and quavery into our second jug of warm wine,
deep in drink & music & poetry infinite
in Williams' old-man clarity of line—

a summer of that on top of a hill in Hayward,
eucalyptus and moon drifting in screenless windows—
every night like that after I quit
my can-plant job, Darrell filling his head
with "finest measures" to carry to Iowa's poem
academy, and me filling my black Bug with beer
& wine, then low-gearing up the hill to Darrell's.

That was a good time and it would last
a few years more before the alcohol
and strange genius got him so he lived
out his string in poverty and half-madness (the Ronald
McDonald glass full with brandy or vodka
quickly drunk and refilled, myriad pills),
declared hapless by our benificent California
and thus supported in the bin and out,
but writing, writing, writing, a "novel," an "epic"
(3 A.M., 3,000 mile phonecalls, loaded,
beginning, "Since I no longer drink . . ." and ending,
"I *am* a poet, I am a very *great* poet . . ."),
all the manuscripts of which, voluminous,
spilling, stepped on, obliterated by wine or vomit,
but heaps and piles of pages, stacks of thick binders—
so said the few friends of sorts who dropped by
his room rarely and with dread those last years—
all the work—what made the life seem less the horror
it was—thrown out, literally shoveled, dumpstered
by the landlord beaten for good out of his rent,
who even had to hose out the room
from the body's lying undiscovered so long,
the blood completely escaped in the final hemorrhage.

The Author

He's carefully counting—five . . .
six . . . eight. Been lots worse, but
he's finding more cracked open,
sweating, half empty, piss-warm
beers about the room where rat-size
roaches flit just out of reach.

But necessary, powerful, urgent
work is brimming this instant,
no time to track down the lairs
of spectral carapaces. Yet noting
how quite precipitously the party-
size Petrov jug has plunged

(so who this morning has defied
his edict: once more let strangers
invade the creative sanctum?),
he determines to abjure vodka,
disdain all—or most—forms of cannabis,
keep the FM transfixed by Mozart,

sleep with his wife (quitting
the cat under the kitchen table),
and finally compose that perfect
poem inscribed on his brain—
everyone will be so proud of him—
instead of the same scrawled wail.

And he finds his calligraphy pen,
dips the nib in Japanese ink,
opens his Moroccan journal
(ages-gone gifts for "The Author
In Our Family"), and blotches down
this latest set of vows,

leaving the pages wedged open
by a fifth of sweet sherry
(20 percent alcohol, cheap
and fast, with a certain
reverse-snob cachet he
chugs with tragedian gusto)

so that tomorrow, discovering
his resolutions in the center
of the gluey desk, he will be moved
by their brave nobility and
not again forget to get started
right away on his new life.

Drinking Buddy

Drunk again the rat in my gut,
mean rat tonight, just two shots
of Russian vodka—molten diamonds
thick from the freezer—and he's back
clawing his favorite vein. On film
he's nothing but a diagnosis
gnawed in gray acid. Only I can see
his scar-pink eyes, jagged whiskers,
his busy, blood-smeared yellow choppers
scoring my stomach wall. For 25 years
no guilt or God, no fears
of hospitals or hearses—
but silty gin, limpid Jameson,
all nights of T'Bird, Ten High, cooking sherry,
rock'n'rye, Yukon Jack, name it.
My rat keeps on rehearsing
his tough-guy act. Sneer perfected
into a cast-iron wound, he demands
another round, bragging how he'll drink me
under the table, under the ground.

Remembering Aunt Tilly

Her dead feet wrapped in bathtowels
seeping purple up to her ankles
set in a plastic bucket
but *not* cut off, those sons of bitches,
under her protests after last year
her chest, by God, they cranked it
open with a rib-spreader
and bypassed death—

Death, tricked again! Hey, Death, *fahngool!*

Then the strokes last month lifted her
out of her squalid apartment—
where her granddaughter's college-boy boyfriend
stored his mountain bike, skis, car parts,
and kenneled the pit bull he won bowling—
lifted and drove her to the nursing home.

Even her secret money vanished then,
"spent down" in a matter of days
at the speed of a grand a week basic fee,
down to her burial policy and a new white dress
stiff with embroidered pearls
to be worn one time and forever.
Medicaid kicked in but the taxpayer
got off easy with Tilly who had worked
all her good years in a line of women
packing lightbulbs off an unstoppable conveyer belt

(the factory rusted and thieved to girders now,
leaching into the viscid Passaic)—

her suffering become her only labor now,
exploited to her last day
for the enrichment of bosses
until the gangrene finally touched her heart.

I write this because Tilly told me to.

Six years ago, just turned 80,
the only sister left,
she drove to Maryland from Newark
for Marie's dying—near 100 degrees
and traffic jammed all down the Turnpike.
She spent day and night at the Frederick hospital,
collapsed in the early morning (a "spell"),
recovered enough in the motel air-conditioning
to leave the next day, back to Newark,
the only white woman for scores of blocks around,
protected by her poverty and strangeness
(how she'd stand on her stoop and yell, "You!
Little nigger boys, run down to the drugstore for me!"
and they'd *do* it) —

back to her street of long-obliterated
fruit stalls and tailors and *pasticcerie,*
but not before telling us "children,"
fiercely, her curse withheld but hovering,
latent power heavy in every breathing word—
Remember your Aunt Tilly!

And each of us she kissed hard
before her grip relaxed.
Ah, no *malocchio* then
darkened her diabetic blue eyes.
And none (cara Matilda!) will I risk now,
howsoever she may be watching.

November Burial

Poor wild zucchini, all summer
I watched you crawl out of the ashpit
toward my window. I'd write a line,
tear out a line, drink more wine, look up
and *there,* you'd crossed another weedpatch,
another deadspot on my starving lawn,
you'd leapt past the cracked birdbath,
past the filigree of swallow bones—
nearer.

At night, I'd turn off the lamp
to see you glowing,
your emerald energy driving
the ground-hum that tuned the crickets,
buoyed the mad moths, kindled the fireflies.
All that rooted power poured
into reaching me, spending yourself
in floppy out-thrusts of tuber and solar-
soaking leaf—so that the little squashes
sprouting along the way
barely gained pubescence. As if blighted
by their first hard-on,
they shriveled.

All summer I waited. You'd soon
be climbing in my window, the whole
enormous length of your following,
your hairy oozing skin,
your massive sun-borne wings—

and we'd dance and writhe
until our marrows mingled.
You got as far as the first cold rain,
as far as the gaunt maple's shadow,
as far as the cat-torn rabbit
glazed with frost.

This morning I was moved toward you.
You were gray, greenlight gone
from dried veins, great leaves shrunken.
I thought of my grandma's transparent cheeks
in the casket. I tried
to lift up your body in one piece
but it turned to bonemeal everywhere I touched,
hollows releasing an arid smoke
past the sweetness of decay.
I gathered you best I could
back to the grave you started from,
and plunged my arms into the heap
until I found your heart,
and lifted it in cupped hands,
an offering of dust held up
to the fugitive sun until
finally it warmed. Then I opened
my hands and your heart
stayed an instant suspended
in air—I saw a prism
of every green
consecrating you in your own dust.

The Man with No Face

May it not be that we can
perceive a thing more truly
by loving it?
　　　Letter to Theo

I

The sun is a nesting swan
upon the burnt umber roofline
of l'hôpital Van Gogh.
Dear Theo—
Oh the fine sun,
it beats on your head
and drives you crazy but
being that already
I just enjoy it.
　　　　　We sweat
in Cinzano shade, Rue des Arènes,
mendicant cats still licking
last night's bull's blood
off their claws. We wait
for Arles' own *primitif;*
The Man with No Face, mouth
like a broken weld, eyes
random as slag, scar-white slate
shattered and re-fused—
the postmodernist tradition.
Or call him a child's chance
découpage, cut with toy tinshears,
impressive work even here
where *les mutilés de la guerre*

get burnished to a high folk art.
Forty years ago he missed de Gaulle's
escape up the Thames, so stayed
to gaze an instant
into the phosphorescent
gloire de France, enough to glaze
and craze him like a Roman urn.

2

This is why we're sweating in
Café des Artistes: in one seared hand
20 Gauloises, in the other
20 new razor blades. He bows, burning
cigarettes curl on his tongue-tip,
vanish into the lipless hole.
He mimes prodigious chewing,
swallows a rat-size bolus,
rubs his belly as if the rat
were real—*ah, c'est très délicieux!*
His immense belch bloats our umbrellas.
Tobacco sheds clot his bared teeth,
ready for close shaving. Now
the unwrapping of the razor blades,
each one a cobalt slice. His tongue
extrudes with magician's flourish,
catches blade after blade,
sliding them down his gullet.
A grin crawls out of his throat.
It says there's nothing as great
as nicotine and steel; try it.
He twirls forefinger at temple, universal
What-me-crazy? gesture, then shakes his head

No-not-crazy because one by one
the blades uncoil upon his tongue.
With his webbed hands he rewraps them
as we applaud and drop
five-franc pieces into his greasy cap.
The cigarettes don't reappear.
                    The Man
with No Face dumps his coins
onto an empty table. There's enough
for his lunch of red wine, enough
for another pack of Gauloises.
Waving to us, he could be
the disinterred Chevalier
jaunting down to his next café.

   3

Oh take The Man with No Face
far out the Rue des Lices, beyond
the leaching brown canal, down
the path of goats and lovers. Lead him
to the scavenged necropolis,
the rubbled lithic park, Alyscamps,
where Vincent waits. Gouged inside
ruined St. Honorat, church of blue
lizards, this prayer: *Suce ma verge,*
c'est extra! Lids of limestone
slide a toenail a year Rhoneward, rotting.
Buy a map from the women knitting
gray hours out of folding chairs
and shawls, buy their warped
cartes postales—black cypresses
spiraling into a driven

yellow heaven, leaves flashing
dun to sheen like new-minted obols
now worth eternal sun-pocked Augusts
in Alyscamps.
       Find exactly where
Vincent set up his easel, composed
his palette in the face
of purple suns slashed by crows,
malachite stars, deep citron, chrome,
emerald and ochre, golden sulphur,
slathered violet and vermillion,
slabbed bitumen, lilac, flesh.
Burning candles
encircle his hat,
heat the light
as Roman sarcophagi flame
into green arks. Ladies and gentlemen
promenade among the tombs,
parasols and frockcoats afire,
the ageless abrasions of the brush.
Here let the faceless man stand,
where Vincent's mistral will sting
blood back into his skull-taut skin,
and create his human features layer
by layer as linden leaves fall
like ripe rain into his open eyes.

La Familia Sagrada

y el verbo se hizo carne . . .
y se habito entre nosotros
(spraypainted in red)

Just off the highway to *las ruinas*
we wait for the jaguar Jesus
and his feathered serpent Maria,
their torn hearts sifting pink dust
within this cinderblock chapel, cool vault
of shadows emerald with lizards
vibrating through the cracks.

Outside, guarding his shop,
the architect sits, earth his pedestal,
the store's stillest statue, praying
or sleeping while mild Mayan blood
now mildews stacks of never-to-be-sold
sarapes, rots processions of blue
and yellow guayaberas, erodes the brown
parade of baked-mud burro cactus planters,
rusts the sequins strung from tilted
pillars of sombreros.
       Los precious?
Quien sabe? Not this Chac Mool, his body
balanced as bedrock, a stone boat of repose,
and smiling, knowing *Las Sagradas* live
forever in his right eye drifting back
toward the little church unnamed and blessed
by no priest but by his own hands, hacked
and broken like hard bread from making

concrete rubble, trucked on his back,
become cathedral walls rising
to a bamboo roof alive with banana leaves
and spiders big as mangos, with paradise
as close as a quick leap of agony into
the jungle thrumming with all God's words—

and smiling, too, because we've just commanded
in our best Spanish Made Simple,
dos coca colas clasicas por favor amigo!,
which arrive warm as noon, foaming sweet,
bottled that instant, for all we know,
by quetzals and kinkajous right behind
the backdoor blanket whose design
is only the known
universe.
Is it his smile that holds us here,
or the vines that have crept up on us
and are wrapping around our legs?
Some ancient drug, it seems, has revealed
destination as childish, hilarious,
despite this heat-slick *ruta* before us,
chopped blade-straight to Belize.
We're staying where the wells cough salt
and cenotes shelter snakes and bats
and electricity flows only from bicycle pedals
and cars run at night without headlights
because the drivers believe they drain power—

because suddenly we know that at any moment
the worthless souvenirs will begin changing—
mute, moldy clay flutes rise

like air-breathing roots, stretch
into fer de lances, vanish through the blanket,
massive mock sombreros turn
into great *tortugas* and *cocodrilos,*
crash off the shelves, heading toward the sea,
plastic Mayan calendar ashtrays blaze up,
burn the stars down to luminous skulls,
mask the sun as a jade panther
with heaven his ballcourt, even the ghostly
Elvis vaquero painted on velvet leaps
onto a wild boar charging into the darkness.

We wait in the chapel, dim with light
raying through the roof. Heaped at the base
of a torn but framed photograph of a girl with a child
are limes, papayas, bananas, split coconuts
rich with flies, and for a second we think:
So the old man's name is Sagrada and here
he sings to his lost wife and dead baby.
But we look up again and see a grown boy
naked, nailed and lashed to a live tree,
and at his feet a woman who must be his mother
resting on green earth, so serene she's
barely breathing, as all around encroaching
her garden swells and bursts with juice and seed
and all its creatures are crying out for each other.

Lost Nest

Your hands cupped
to its woven weight,
a heft resistless, less
than twigs and dry grass,
less than its four
milky gray eggs, shells
so thin the blood-sacs
mottle through to
rust-flecks, eggs small
as an infant's testicles—

its fragile wattling
exposed on a mud wheeltrack.
One more step and
you'd crush it, even as
cats, snakes, magpies
close in for the kill,
deep, wet grass all around,
but no one with any notion
how to move it, sooner
transplant a womb—

and less than the sounds
spent to this point,
each syllable a vanishing,
until only that eyeblink's
footfall withheld,
the circlet's frail defiance,

dark speeding randomness
minutes behind, are balanced
in your hands, unharmed if now
you stop, set it down.

Crofter Tea, Skye

Pig-squeal of scalded milk
piped into tea. Nothing but breath
and slant rain congealing on
two sheep-bladder windows.
A kettle
swung above earth-fire.
A hard bed for birth,
love, death, waking. A fiddle,
and a Bible in an outlawed language.
The low lintel
oiled black by head-knocks
of men too sure the world
would always be their size.

Count only on tea twice boiled,
strength summoned from dregs;
and four walls, greasy as live wool,
so unresisting the iron wind
slides round them even while gulls
beat backwards and the three-hour sun
is stripped of light.

Wisely did they
in Gaelic or Pictish or Norn sing
their terror of winter. It petrifies still,
like the Bog People—a song
of ice-broken boulders
rooted in abandoned hillsides,
silent as the last glacier's scree

except where a chimney
has collapsed into a dolmen,
or a *ceilidh* floor
has upthrust a cairn.

The Day of the Donkey

I

Ben Bulben, hacked stump
of the island's first tree,
once ringed by giants,
a gnarly swift climb
to heaven (ere the craze
for bloody barefooting
up stony Croagh Patrick),
felled now, low to the world,
flat as a Drumcliffe grave—
leaches lime through skulls
of elk and kings, gullies rain
far enough to wash this slab:
his trough of pebbles picked over
like Killarney postcards while
horsemen, bleary-eyed, disguised
in coachdriver's motley, lean
at ease, idling, smoking, knowing
the tour's last "sight" comes next—
"That clump of trees. No, not on shore.
Look, on the lake. *That's* the isle
of his famous poem."

They recite
line one; light cigarettes.

I beat their buses out of the carpark,
but Lough Gill's thrashing in squall,
churning up leaden fish, so I say no

to the rowboat's pilgrimage. I've lost
the lines of his lyric anyway,
but take an artful photo—a young
Polish priest, waving, his grin soft
through sheeting mist, who'd never heard
of Innisfree. Three oar-strokes,
and he's at speed, crushing waves.

A desire beyond actions undone
strokes my shadow's skin, brushes
its lips. My map unfolds like flesh.

2

Still a hard day's run to reach
A chill's sway-back bridge—
mossy rust, rubbly droppings
salted by a flooding tide—

and already I can kiss the feet
of those famine graves: legend
I quaffed from pints' umber crowns
deep to amber scum; deciphered

from bartop spillage-runes
back in some Sligo liars' pub:
of starved ghosts singing as they sank,
bards to the bone, under a hungry swale.

For there's the castle, skeletal
landmark to that tale, rising now
against slant light, huge in my sight
as those ditches bunged with corpses.

But donkeys are guarding the sound—
hirsute trolls clopped up
from the bridge's rotted pilings,
hawing at me to pay the toll.

Their lead beast veers at me,
a mud momentum bulking fast
toward where I'm too astonished
to crank up the window.

Within a spumous halo of blue
botflies, he thrusts his whole
braying, swaying dolmen of head
into the car, fills it

with his nostrils, ears, lips,
his iron teeth, his black
and wild eyes—slobbering breaths
so stenched the flies turn green.

I fend him off with my lunch,
my graveside picnic-to-be—
petrified soda bread, brick

3

and duck away from his grinding,
his donkey bristle burning
when he swings his skull
like a sledge against my face.

I'm sure, given time, I'll charm this scene,
deal the snapshots like blackjack,

til even I believe my anecdote *asinus:*
how that creature, drooling love,
nuzzled me, breathed earth upon me,
knew me in those donkey-deep eyes
that gazed me away from that
for which I'd come: knew the dead
would never whisper hints why I'm alive
nor chant me to any place I'll find
where I was lost.

In truth I am enraged,
a Celt forestalled, spit-globbed,
and unfed! Driving (driven) off,
I fear my treasured tragedy—
sea-fog pooling, salt as tears,
in unmarked concave stones,
their lone alcoholic orphan,
buried deeper than his drunken father,
instantly ancestral, sickened
by the liquor of self-pity,
yet his quest hardly mock
for all his "Irish" bravura fists
and verse trembling like sick muscles—
fear this quaint catastrophe
must dwindle fast, its prose at best
an epilogue. I seethe back inland,
track more slane-cut than paved,
mucking its way through bog.

No, a plague
on oracular donkeys—and curse
those melodramatically black

potatoes, bard-sung heroes hot
with whiskey-brag, turf-fire's
hissing rank smoke
like uncorrupted odor
off a saint's wristbone,
and the rest of it: "loovelly" tearooms,
tumbled crosses and cairns,
eternal "soft day" rains—all,
save the mad music of the poems.

4

My imprecations cloud the sky—
or clouds cloud? I can't tell,
Darker than any dusk my hell
whenever it's so pleasure-lit.

But if pain endures
as life's bedrock, now let
its boulders break ground,
each sculpted roughly, simply
by martyrs, monks, poets, poteen,
in the slow sharding of sheer beauty.
They calm, they rearrange
like standing stones;
carve crumbly turf into a ring
of memory but greenly known.

North-lasting light promises
a roof, a plate of scones: enough,
though I swear to devour a leprechaun
if I reach Ballina before full night.
Then earth flames

an upside-down false dawn
that lets me find a slim,
freshet-fed waterfall
leaping the road's cut, free
of mud-marsh and weed-slime.
The wheel turns me toward it.

I wash the donkey's crusted foam
from my hands and face.
It tastes sweet, Salt cleanses my eyes.
Under that stream of liquid ice
I chill the wine I've saved.
The sun is diving west, pulled
by the same old crimson coursers . . .
But no, askant I see this sun is sped
by a team of fire-winged donkeys,
and mine is flying to the lead,
his mud burnt gold.

Mass at Rathmullen

Through enclosures of cows & sheep
above & below, climbing stiles or slipping over
stones tumbled from moss-slick & donkey nosing—

they come, stepping creaky on canes or leaping
each other across the cattle-guard grate,
solemn converging, caps pulled off, scraping boots—

huge displays of nose-blowing, coughing, wheezing
& ten minutes late the joking loud then hushed,
Mongoloid children in arms, overbig, whining & whooping—

smell of hangovers thick as wool,
old men alone, faces blasted red, never to heal,
young men like kneeling boulders, mumbling whiskey prayers—

muck-pants, unraveling sweaters, gone-at-elbows jackets,
women with 6 or 8 children under the age of ten,
shawls unwound, coats steaming, dresses new-pressed & rain-slack-

the priest jumbles Irish-English & Latin, forgetting:
Now this part is the division or multiplication, no
the division . . . the loaves or the fish . . . *and* the fishes—

the frail boy, ears blue, hands & eyes clenched in prayer,
knees hard on the rail, indented with devotion,
behind him his Mongoloid brother kicking & mewling.

To Find the Standing Stones at Kenmare, Go . . .

I

not far along a tilting terrace row
all flaking stucco, stipple-patches
of pinkish grey, verdigris-scaled
pale salmon, even still
some burnt-gold glowingness
unpeeled from the shadowed walls,
housebacks turned against the sun's
plunging past crooked Kerry's end—
rust-frozen gates mishung,
roses gone wild as cats,
jags of broken windows polished
by winds unslowed through empty rooms . . .

2

and beyond the inevitable potter
(this island surviving as crafts fair),
children held up like cameras
to see her at her wheel,
fondling mind to mud to shapely
emptiness, slicking the spinning
hole to hold the tourists' teabags,
or cattails, painted pebbles,
pocket change, sneezy potpourri,
but never for them the proper
misty brew of cider and poteen . . .

3

then on by the hall with its ancient
blazonry—CINEMA—lost across a cracked
concrete front, overlayered by the
fading HAND-LOOMED CARPETS AND RUGS,
where in back now in dim light,
below a screen so torn and stained
a moment's riffling fills it again
with magical embodiments, flourishes
the current avatar: some sort
of mini-car chopshop, thicker shadows
muffling steel-on-steel shrieking and
the hissing of the cutting torch—
so even tearing engines apart
and body-fender hammering seem scenes
in an eroding sculpture, earthen art,
funerary lore passed down, bone
to bone, by the bog-giants' guild . . .

4

now right at the green garage door,
bright-beaded (rain the only newness),
where the signpost's arrows point
back and up and there and there,
salt-eaten runes driven anywhere
by the berserk coursers of the air,
right before the once black and white
terrier, mongrelized by time, watcher
since the invention of plaster—
but *not* five paces farther where
the Lost end up in the missus's tearoom,
fire-soothed, dry, delectating a tray

of recumbent scones, breathing slow
into a smoking cup, butter melting,
gooseberry jam dripping, legs easing,
true mission entirely forgotten . . .

5

but, no, that escaped, take
the hoof-churned muck-track
beginning just beyond the long
cross-barred gate (for wet cows
to slick their heads through)
behind the green garage (the lock's
never locked, nothing says "Keep Out"),
and follow the path down into
a sudden lumberyard where, swung
high above the timber piles warping
from weight of their own sweetness,
chain-muscled claws at winch's end
drop and close on four, no three,
now two, or one log luckily
dangling from the teeth, airborne
away toward the saw-sound rising
from an unseen mill toward which
the track is sluicing all debris . . .

6

and end it here, if that's sufficient
foolishness, for one person's stone
circle is another's God-cursed field,
and, after all, most of the starred
celebrity lithic sites, dolmens, barrows,
portals to ashpits, have been checked off

in *Michelin,* neat as velvet ropes—
and were these Kenmare "monoliths,"
nameless in all the guidebooks,
literally stumbled across in what was
our previous lifetime, ever really *here?*—
were they just imagined, saved like a crow's
bent feather in an old cracked-spine
journal book at the page that tried
to hold how Skellig skewered the sky
and shocked it blue beyond thought,
or just *needed,* a reason for returning? . . .

   7

so enough of this slogging, slipping
and pulling each other down slithering
in the too-fertile mud, boots sucking
and squishing, shivers setting in,
the thick odor of sawdust mounds
jelling—enough to climb one of these
pulpy humps and peer through rain
and heavier water rolling off
hopeless hats (perhaps the whole island,
our day's run west, the sour cheese and
iron bread in the one-pub village
that no one had ever left or returned to,
their sullen, embarrassed silence hard
at the stranger until the first dumb question
is ventured and then the stories and laughing
flow with the Harp and it will cost
the new friend a bloody nose to buy a drink—
perhaps this entire journey
is a chimera or will be: some postcards

of impossible vistas, some antique poems,
absurdly musical, recovered from
an improbable tongue, a journal full
of lies)—enough just to see the path
accelerate down the bruised gleaming
of the machine-gouged slope, gathering rain
and speed into a newborn torrent, force
spent spuming over a low cliffedge,
purpling the whisper-wide, deep-cutting
River Finnerty, wind-clean and black
with pitch of the island's last pines . . .

8

yes, turn back, salvaging the image,
for memory only cannot disappoint,
while rain's aiming little steel fishes,
and clamber on powerful flipper-arms
up the cutbank slime to gain
solid purchase, short retreat
to the car—but this rotted barbed wire,
this ruined stile do seem familiar,
and the stench of sheep shit, density
of winter fog, lifting from self-made bowls,
overwhelms all the rest, like memory,
forces up the eyes to the near horizon
a nose away, and there they are . . .

9

the stones,
corpse-gray but lambent, sculpted by
five thousand years, here tumbled, scarcely
non-random but for anything like a circle's

rarity outside the brain's corolla or
the galaxies', rest half-buried, fallen
as from the sky, like the hacked parts
of a dismembered god, flesh turned to rock,
veins to roots and lichens, but shoulder,
neck, buttocks, thigh and knee, heel, tongue,
breasts, eye-holed head still thrust and
arch and shrug and swell around the center—
the lowest stone, a smooth convexity like
a baby's belly but really the perfect curve
of vulva or glans—and the sheep, dumb sheep
at a kneel taking the silvery wind and rain,
make breathing stones too, perhaps a square,
or a sprung rectangle of Sleeping Sheep—
except for the one that's straying near
what must be the fist, the youngest
spring-shorn one, now rubbing its naked
green-striped rump joyously
against the cracked knuckles, as if
to scrape off the dye, to mark
the coupling sun and moon, or zenith
of a white-bearded star, or merely
the traveler's final stumble—the ripe
and plumply scrawny one, with sheepchild eyes,
head lifted, waiting for the sacrifice,

Salcombe Ramble

What fold-cracked, rune-blotched map
tricked us onto such a trail
as gullied to gravel and fell

dead over the cliff? We'd begun
our half-day's whistling trek
to morning's soft horizon, stoked

with red-eyed eggs, bony ham,
split tomatoes, Wonder bread—
all thick-fried in freshest lard—

boiled "oat-nuts," and cold toast
limp in its rack, served in health
by the crocheted lady whose garden path

led us by the hand up from that faint
map-dot, Salcombe, just when the bay sighed,
trembled, seethed—and sped out Bolt Head.

And suddenly through shredding mist
a glistering meadow of mud appeared.
Then—the moment landmarks lustered

and dissolved, Striding Man's fingerpost
tempting us tamely inland,
the true way veering from our mind—

a shingly ford surfaced for us. Slimy
tide-weeds lay across the inlet's gleam,
and we skated its slick to find our climb.

First hour, we slipped up shale greased
with smouldering droppings, welcomed
at top by a dappled colt who bloomed

a shyly swaying erection as he ran
to chomp our clumps of wild carrot—
oh, Adam and maiden, all that, but not

the hobbity amble we'd thought. Somehow
we'd forked far off from the ideal,
and felt pain leaking like stony gruel

from hips, knees, corroding backs:
an aching like antique flails
threshing the brain. Only golden hills

of hay kept us climbing, mirage-like
barnshade luring us. Our prayers flew
up to those sumptuous bales of straw

we envisioned pitched high, rising
unto sleeping bats and fattest flies—
O let them be there. One last wheeze,

and we collapsed on chaff (vision true,
even to botflies' slow, smaragdine
tumbling), As our bodies' brine

scaled to chafing sweat, we fed
each other warm apples, and cheese
so heated it gave off haze—

and slept a little, enough at least
to wake to looping bats, early owls
chanting as from the Western Isles,

and chills. We climbed again,
the world's brink in sight, a blank
scarp-edge where days darken and sink—

and did not stop climbing until,
exhausted as the light, we rolled
over the last uncharted stile

and, feet curved to stone, leaned
deep toward the boulder-scree'd
fields flowing down to the sea,

and watched the Channel turn slate
and break up into monsters.
The sun furled violet before us.

Then we could never be hotter—
we steamed like driven cattle,
our joints burning a gritty oil,

the last mile fighting a gristle
grinding freefall track—until it eased
to the walk we'd imagined we chose

that long-ago morning. Once more
we smelled that fish-ripe, shining muck,
though the bay, storm-pushed, *had* come back,

and mud-stuck gasping dinghies now
were swimming. One yawed through foam
and rocked us across under thunder—"home"

to the war-widow's tea-dusty room.
Her astonished lace curtains
writhing to the quickening rains,

we scraped off salt-thick clothes
and naked, face to face, lay sated,
cooling, as the dark harbor rose.

The Last Time

Remember the moist blue breeze
brushing us through tall doors swung
full open onto the brave *balcone*
flung far over the shadow-cut canyon
widening to hold the sea that leapt
green fire, the horizon jagged violet.

For a week we warmed that little room
impossibly tenoned to cliffstone
high above Santa Marguerita's crescent harbor—
late afternoons, shouts of men at *bocce,*
rising pure, from the maw of the cleft,
translated into miniature bells.
And did *our* cries ring dark, deep below?

That last time is gone, but I hope
it began with our climbing down
that knotted rope of a road, hungry
for one more long *colazione* . . . but to find
the dockside bolted from its doze, atremble,
for Mastroianni, life burnt golden-ripe
at the end of his ultimate season, this moment
promenades the shade-striped piazza!—

and let me imagine we broke
our bread atom by atom, as if tearing
the crust of our only day,
finishing just this one, then just one more
bowl of quivery, lemony mussels,

each enfolding a parmesan pearl,
while behind us *il padrone* kept flicking
chance crumbs of Time off empty tables—

until *basta!* (the sky cooling, paling
to raw dough), we wound our tiny car
back up the mountain where the sun
still spilled over the crest. And in
that recovered hour of hot, thin light,
oh didn't we give the seagulls, planing
the abysmal space below our bed,
all their reason for screaming?

If only then—before the gray scar
wrinkled up from my pubic bone—
if only then I'd known
mere minutes so prodigally held
our finale, oh, I'd now recall
my every stroke toward absolute depth,
your every drive toward infinite openness,
and how our eyes met in the heat
of our slow and gasping spasm-song.

A Matisse Odalisque

reclines on her chaise longue, knees wide,
thighs relaxed by seduction no warmer

than their own firmness under crimson
pants ballooning up from mid-calf, fold

upon fold flowing the narrowing v to her
crotch: red darkens, streaks chrome-yellow—

then luxuriance of belly, a curved umber
burnished from gold (if fat at all,

revealing the little girl who stole
raw, sweet dough when her mother

bent away, coughing), and the torso's
in-tapering rise to her breasts, rondures

mounded by mere supineness, not depending
or pendulous but essential to her whole

composition: nipples perfectly off center,
rosettes against the pink-cream skin—

and bare ankles, too, and naked feet
casually crossed (would uncross in an instant),

and arms splayed back, wrists caught in
twisting tulle behind her head, elbows erect,

shameless as her knees, *all* an offering!—
as are these words upon desire upon paint

upon flesh upon a young woman upon time.
The removes multiply, and break your heart.

Still she lies at ease, yet now, since a
minute's passed, *braced* (can you see sinews?)

on her sturdy, insatiable chair, a meaty
pea-green affair (maroon blotches hide stains?).

She looks only at you, and when you look back
her pose shifts: the belly sucks in,

refirms, breasts lift, legs open even more,
her navel suddenly unfolds like a vulva,

and for all her worldliness, that
voluptuous poise, mouth too magenta

quite to smile, she's maybe 18, her calmness
a melting vacuity, pure repose

swirling to envelop any man—or woman—
sufficiently careless to join the picture.

Her world's a bed sagging with longing;
Go in, the draperies will turn transparent—

your seed will vanish to sequins,
your clear oils lighten to wine. Come in,

taste the very liquor of your yearning—
and the artist's too, who all the days

and nights his hands possessed full power,
slid them everywhere over and into the secrets

of his subject, discovering here all *he* knew.
Now, go, before you waste all her desire—

before her perfume leaks through canvas cracks
and houris rush to hide her in black cloaks.

Tin Whistle

Crickets winding October's rusty winch,
ratchet of woodpeckers in slate rain,
acorns thudding the loamy roof,
creek high, running clean—

only the mind at any remove,
as if packed in cosmoline, in the dark
of its own greasy glow, no grip
on any of it, some kind of crude tool:

cartesian hand-axe, or the gods' portable
slit-trench (patent ever pending)
with its rarefied stench rising
from labors as silent as the sun—

or at best a bent tin whistle, again
and always this cheap, shiny present
from the addled great-aunt
to her ever-bored birthday boy,

that wall-bound, window-bound pup
who tries a few mischievous tootles,
then drops it on the heap
of scrap-songs that fill his room—

while outside all the feathered,
fanged, milk-bleeding crickets
are outwailing rocks and cracking
into music more syllables than stars.

Enisled

J'ai supprimé . . . tous les adjectifs.
"Joseph Grand"

Lunch lingers—garlicky lamb
in full gambol, leaping tongue
to tongue as insatiate young
papillae quiver—until becalmed

gourmands stretch toward shore
and girls slip thin "tops" back on,
boys floating next to them. Another
evening waits upon the pier—again,

in a haze of murmurs, smiles, all
reboard for the little ferry's cute
whistling back to weight and soot.
They wave to us, *adieu!*—when the squall

on schedule, a ritual riffling blow,
resinks the boat. We hear no cries:
dusk melts in the toy lake like snow,
water smoothed by an ancient breeze.

2

So we are left enisled, perfumed
breaths and lifespans lost
since we rose from bus exhaust,
leapt long over the continuum

of Engine, and the waterborne
bois opened like lips.
Gilt menus, silver, soft linen
offered, accepted—crystal cups

spilling honeyed light. Oh, how
to consume the same still day,
since dawn drinking way,
way too much Monet? We show

clearly classic signs of *musée*
excess: arguing Sisley really
outsizzles Cezanne, going phobic
at the Old Man's Friend, entropy,

and counting drifts of "gray ones,"
aged youths, skin that scoured color,
that pre-ataxic pewter, hung
on lovers' arms, a last fair hour

to gain the condition of music,
the orchestra insane. In short,
some new strong-force has worked
this salon into *natures mortes*—

and we the dark matter
sifted here, sufficing as filler:
the busy decor between pictures.
But if, just maybe, we order

some immense dessert, a viscid
climax of cake, cream, syrup
flowing as a child envisions
life inside his belly (let's hope

some waiter still attends us!),
our breaths might only rise,
even while bony chests collapse
in some alternate universe.

   3
Then, dusted by the solar mist
mottling through acer leaves,
golden lads, with all we've wished . . .
but that naked girl's body

arcs up from the grass,
taut ease upon her elbows, warm
clouds her attire—and formed
by her braced upper arms
a burnished shadow, dark wreath
triangling depth, where, new
yet full, her breasts depend
a whisper above the earth

whose iron desire curves them.
Not sex excites us: but quick
perfection, moment uncomplex
as hunger, and the question

if beauty can at all exist
outside of what we try to save,
hidden on this pulsing island
dividing particle from wave.

Paris: Le Chalet des Iles

Healing

for Joanne

Your back bruised to radiance,
swollen glow pulsating
at the base of your spine,
spreading smears of purple,
maroon, dirty gold—you could turn
onto only one side. Week after week
I watched the raging colors crawl,
lying to you, "It's looking better."

I wished my hand could turn to moss,
to feather, to frailest breath, so you
would not cry when I rubbed your back
with the bean-oil that our dear
witch-friend swore would calm
and cure the maddened energies.
I only glazed the pain, shined it hard
as you trembled and gasped *Good!*

If only I could have suffered it,
somehow entered you and taken all
you'd give me of it. So *one* we'd been
in pleasure, but yet apart in this?
Trying to believe, I aimed my mind
until I imagined a tiny moon's corona
cooling and shrinking the jagged
edges of that broken, bloody light.

But still you hurt too much for me
to even hug you, for me even
to move next to you in bed—
so I slept on the floor
on my straw of four cracked ribs,
and listened to you moan through the drugs
and whimper when you tried
to reach the bedpan on your own.

Then one day you could get up
for the bathroom, refusing my help
to lift you onto and off the toilet.
You'd use only "Alice,"
your aluminum walker—each step
bought with agony. The worst
was the wiping, which you
sobbingly let me do.
Our witch-friend kept phoning me:
"You have to *love* her ruined back. That's
your wife now—that's where her life
is struggling to live. You *must*
see beauty there. A two-ton automobile
ground it to burger-meat, and only you
can love what's left of that poor
precious aura. I'm *telling* you."

. . .

Now, a year later, I stroke
the puffy fist just above your ass.
Softened to rose and blue, it holds
the pain where I can hide it

under my palm. And my groin takes in
its gray, steady heat as I spoon-hug
up to you, fitting again (and prodding;
sorry, can't help that). We're drifting

into deep afternoon. We never believed
in the mystical oil, our witch's
wonder salve. But love? What fool
still feels witchcraft lurking there?
Except in truth I loved you for a year
more than I could bear, loved the
ugliest of you, all I couldn't share,
though I'd sooner have slathered my raw

nerves with your suffering than make
myself love it. Ah, now the house again
exhales the alchemic soul of your own
miraculous *marinara* sauce, as we linger
abed, satiated and hungry, windows
filling with violet. And I am always
silently casting my spell, *Be here, be whole* . . .
holding us closer than you can know.

Our Life on the Floor

for Joanne

Remember, Joanne, our life on the floor?—
that cheap-apartment-yellow wall-to-wall
linty rendezvous when gravity, our friend,
eased us down onto beanbags and pillows,
all essentials within lithe leaning distance:
the "stereo"—turntable with quarters
taped to the "tone-arm" to weight it
against bouncing too much when we danced,
volume stuck on "10," vibrating speakers
facing from opposite walls as monumental
as the hollow stone Delphic goddesses
through whom the ancient oracles sang—
our "albums" lined upright, edges outward
along the baseboard, the month's selections
lost in stacks, strewn about (my first
"To Do" list starting without my knowing it:
I'd better organize these albums pretty soon),
our separate "collections" beginning to mix,
the life-saving duplicates pairing up—
Nina Simone, Stevie Wonder, Dylans,
Sinatra, Procol Harum, Ray Charles, more
and more that over and over played
the same prayerful song lifting above
the particular music: called *Can This Be?,*
or to state its full title, *Can This Be What
Enduring the Lonely Drift, the Insistence to Not
Quite Be Killed or Go Insane These Terrible
Decades of Assassinations, Riots, War,*

Hatred, and Stupidity, HAS BEEN FOR?
Maybe . . . we think, yes . . . maybe, yes, yes,
here it's happening, the miraculous
unheard-of rumored impossible thing we now
are creating each out of the instant and
only to give it to the other so as to be
replenished by the other—as Coltrane's *A Love*
Supreme flowed over the solid floor (mind-high,
heart-high) of that old house in an old city
neither of us, unaware of the other, remotely,
at such distance could even imagine a year before
we'd ever set foot in much less find
our life in

2

Now, my lovely Joanne,
my hamburger helpers and tuna casseroles
simmered and seethed in readiness for you
on that greasy two-burner stove (just as
my dessicated soul warmed to where I
could imagine chewing some sustenance from it).
Ah, we ate so well, especially after dinner
when the floor, like the Nile in flood,
brought whatever next we needed.
The roach clip?—lost, but here it is!
The little one-eared TV?—blind, abuzz,
a screenful of zapping, but here it drifts
in view with clarity of Mary Tyler Moore,
Carol Burnett, Newhart (O genii of first
hip and innocent incarnations!).
And the mattress, that sumptuous Goodwill
luxury barge, fabulously appointed with

a sheet, that every night (if not afternoon)
floated up to us, tumbled us aboard—
and oh we rode it until that lumpy bulk
levitated and *flew,* a wavy flying carpet
propelled by endless soft collisions.
Then I'd tell you stories and
you'd tell me stories, about far-off lands
called *California* and *Italian* and
each other, remembering, foreknowing,
inventing (the first poem I wrote for you:
the moon, our private trembling light,
centered in the open window, suspended
in a Rousseau-blue night, buoy bells
off Spa Creek deepening the silence)—
our continuous description, impossible to pause,
of the one life we were becoming (you say
you knew; to me it was ignorant joy, immanence).
Was this the Love & Peace so long
marched for, invoked at close of letters,
phonecalls, visits, asserted on bumper stickers
and buttons, swayed to in concerts, rallies,
happenings, drunk to, toked to, tripped after,
chanted, mantra'd, poems by the thousands thrown
into flames for? Were they simply *here,*
the love and peace, the love, the peace,
the you, the me, the us? Yes—
and all on the floor!

3

Then we had nothing, unless we count
your endtables suitable to be used
as footstands for performing elephants,

and my one *objet:* the red plastic rose
inserted in a green flagon of slowly
etherealizing Hai Karate. Add your vicious dog,
add my little linear tales and Nancys,
and our old cheap cars psychedelically named,
and your clunker typewriter you *sold* me,
ripped me off for ninety dollars!
What else? Some dishes, a sheepskin throwrug,
my binder of mostly pretty badly stoned poems,
our books, the student standards plus
your Kahlil Gibran, Browning, and occult guides,
my two hardcovers: Roethke's slim *Collected*
and James Agee's Shakespearian sharecropper song.
But really we had
nothing really
except each other.
(Even a few years later,
married, settled homeowners—
having scraped up $2,500 down between us—
trying to grow a bush and some roses
in the raw clay in front of our "semi-detached,"
dazed owners of a new Datsun, 5-grand with radio—
even then we would be *en vacances*
in a Jersey shore motel, the ice machine exhausted,
when the TV told us Elvis had died.)

Now we have several
of most everything—
a mini-Pitti Palace
with crew and staff on call,
seven sofas, more than some sultans,
uncountable TVs and VCRs,

many rugs that came with appraisals,
rugs that blinded whole villages,
rooms with names like the Morning Room,
the Media Room, the Lounge,
cars that confer great prestige upon us,
that teenagers gaze after in wonder and longing.
Our dilemmas are "London or Paris or Rome??"—

such quandary! And how to most cleverly swap,
as in "Monopoly," our luxury condos for
equally posh units in other fabulous realms,
And wonderful as may be
our revels and our pageant,
we really have
nothing really
except each other.

I seem, my most dearest, to be telling you
this news, letting you in on something.
But of course we know it was you
who let me in. I had nothing,
period, until you. It's true—
only then, with you, did I have *anything*,
which suddenly was *everything* because
you gave me love, a world, life.
And this too I'll say—
I'm glad you showed me it's OK
to have a bed, a chair, and more
to raise us a little space above the floor!

When She's Gone . . .

She'd like to be stuffed
and raven-haired set among us,
goblet of opalescent *beaujolais*
poised in her right hand, dark prism
for the sun's surrendering afternoon.
She'll wait upon your every word,
and if you chance to say something graceful and true
you might discern her smiling,
eyes alive with some sudden aureolate memory,
approval glowing in the room's amber shade—
and then an attar so subtle, so elusive,
as of a blossom that dies at a touch,
that ever after you'll scent it
in only your most mindless erotic frenzies.

Though reticent to a fault,
she'll occasionally with mildest insistence prefer
a crystal bowl
of Orville Redenbacher's Gourmet Popping Corn.

And later after charming chatter
of old friends' failures and follies,
of golden summers in Tuscany, of secret cafés
in Paris and Provence and Barcelona,
of the season's best-built baseball players—
we'll remark how penumbral
the afternoon's become, how abruptly chill,
how quickly the day has passed,
how pure pleasure *does* make it run.

Ah, now, the guests take their leave.
They touch your cheek, your lips, your open hand,
begging you not to rise. And you don't.
They sing from their touring cars,
"Goodnight, Love, *adieu,*
sweetest of sweet dreams! We'll call you!"

Then, at last,
it's just you and I!
I disinter
our most magical weed,
put on endless tapes
of *Geraldo* and *The Simpsons,*
and roll us a giant Aztecan joint
to last us til morning.
An eruption
of tropical flame and smoke—
and your left arm unbends
and the flaky crust
of your fingers falls away
as their bones deftly clutch.
Your lungs creak, gasp, groan, expand.
Spring wine splashes upon
your chaste ivory gown
as you rise toward me.
Oh, all your reserve
melts away *now,*
my Lovely!

Old Poet

for William Stafford

Language dims like the eyes,
sky whitens, river fades
underground. Breath of gold-
tipped wild hyacinths rooted
in a mossy granite jag,
ice-spray of newborn waterfall,
fragilities driven like mist
to another world
whose distance holds all
we can see: a prairie, then,
say a Kansas, great burn-over
greening under star-shadows,
horizon unreachable yet cragged
with seventy-years' memory:
slope-shouldered stones
huge as mountains or children,
tilting, toppling, rising,
worn names freshly carved
by the rocks' splitting.
Such distance drains
our fretful mirrors.
All our querulous, trivial,
lapidary jade-work gone
at his simple whispered *Why?*
A hard, blue morning wind
still does circle this world,
binding blowing cottonwoods
to glacier-scoured plains,

human heart to ropy veins,
a man's sweet voice
to a few love songs.
It says: *Whatever stays,*
belongs.

Amends

Someday, I thought, if she got old enough,
her memory at last wept out, I'd let
her read my poems. Then their crude-cut lines
might seem some other woman's scars—those years
their images relive, just bad TV,
a series with no characters to like,
no plot or humor, crap writing, and yet
it ran and ran, somehow impossible
to cancel, for it was her only show,
that '50s classic of banality,
needing no audience but her and me.

I'd hear it from my room, as many walls
away as I could get, wakening to
its rising theme: his knuckles bashing her
like tired, slow, prolonged applause, while I
turned tiny, atomizing into rays,
and streamed up to my real home on Mars.

I never ever told her that I wrote,
hoping to spare us both such sorrow as
my doleful "mother poems" bled like love—
so waited, waited. Someday she'd forget
the alcohol, shame, anger, fear, despair:
his steady violence monsterizing me,
seeping like toxic fog into my soul
until I sprouted fangs and rougher fur
than his.
Someday his fists would simply keep

the beat behind some lush, crescendoed score
for her life's movie starring her as Her.

Now someday has arrived. She's getting fit
at 84 to go to heaven, where
there's surely an eternity of tears,
infinities of woeful paradise
to vindicate her life spent sobbing. But,
merely white noise in the dim Sunrise Home,
her weeping doesn't wrench hearts here. Harassed,
indifferent "aides" spit mad non-English in
her face, while her gray son floats off, his voice
a dribbly smear of light. Why won't he *talk?*

Words rot in uric air. she'll never know
the nightmare poetry I made of her,
compulsively, the vision of her bruised,
beseeching face before me, crying down
the years. My telling her don't worry, how
I'll get a gun and next time shoot him, *Bam,*
and get a job and get us out of here—
just as his junker car coughs dead outside,
and me, at ten or twelve or fourteen, caught
again without that dreamed-of gun, afraid
of grease-black creases, hard as welded hate
he makes by clenching corded hands as if
around a steel bar and raising them
like huge sledges above my head, terror
strong as up-rushing whiskey puke I knew
the scald of even then when drunkenness
protected me, no matter if she fled.

I fear that if I show her one, she'll ask
if I have more, and then I couldn't stop
from reading her the heap, her Ur-sitcom
laugh-tracking waves of stark bewilderment
as all her trite catastrophes rush back,
the wacky punchlines of her wretched life—
as close as I could come to beating her
with open hands, shouting at her, as at
a wailing child, *Come over here and you'll
get something real to cry about.*

        No, though
I owe her most for this weird calling, she
must never know I am a poet, lest—
switching dementias—she picks a new
channel and suddenly demands to hear
the *nicest* poem she's inspired. I know
that instant I would find, in poisonous
bop prosody, my Failed Poem—rant
scrawled down, destroyed, unspoken all my life,
the dream too terrible for memory;
but finally then would hold, as in a phial,
perfected distillate of rage and grief,
and pour it deep into her deafened ear,
special for her.
        Oh, I'm supposed to make
direct amends to everyone I've harmed,
yet cause no harm, but any line could kill.
Invisibility and silence, then,
must serve as they have done for fifty years:
hide every page where words unwritten sing
mute pain. There is no poet, and his book
stays blank.

Halloween: An Oncology

I   INPATIENT

So I've become, at last, "my kind of thing,"
irony sharpened to the decimal
(seven-point-four, in fact). Visitors bring
metallic LUV balloons that pray GET WELL,

prayer coffee mugs and praying daisies; then
my prayer joke: the mumbling kid who stands
like Bartleby, lank seminarian
on his first training mission, dangling hands

from hairy wrists too long for cuffs, black hair
thick below knuckles, starveling boy of God,
remote, preferring not to take a chair,
deep into "vigiling." I try to prod

the Lord out of him. "Tell me, Reverend,
do you enjoy your work?" He nods awake,
moves, haltingly, bedside: here is one friend . . .
your *best* friend . . . wept, bled, died . . . all for your sake"—

my cue to turn the TV up. My Show
is on, my marathon romancer: one
life to live, children all, restless, they know
they're young, too beautiful for cancer. Fun

forever is their plague; they swell, sweat, seethe.
Whether their play stars Lust or Hate, they must

endlessly lubricate and heavy-breathe
since bold electrons don't mutate to dust.

One dear friend smuggles in a Siamese fish—
"a *fighting* fish," she whispers hard—a red
prostate-sized glob. It vibrates like my wish
this weren't happening. By week's end it's dead.

And so much more—oh, such well-meaningness!—
ten self-help books (subtext: *it's your bad choice*),
five crystal amulets, one noxious mess
of Chinese carry-out, the confused voice

of my mother 3,000 miles away
asking should she come out and help (no, *please!*),
an orange styrofoam cacti display,
and pamphlets laying odds on my disease.
(*Not* on this list: a pretty nurse's shy
and tender cleansing 'round my catheter;
the friend who reads me his new work—we try
always for the perfected; my wife, her

mere presence *all* the gift, what frightens me
to lose.) But one last lump of anti-cheer—
close pals, knowing my "thing," all guarantee
the payoff: "Dave, you've got a great poem here."

For I've achieved some minor ill-repute
as sentimentalist of the grotesque.
Deformity is my ideal of *cute*;
sweet Pity chains me to my writing desk—

but not this time. I won't take any notes,
and painkillers I hope obliterate
all images. Words uttered by white coats—
entering, exiting—encode my fate.

2   OUTPATIENT

My language, like white coals, dwindles, burns out,
and I don't give a shit, except to swear
this thing is not what I will write about.
Which resolve holds until a festive air

vaguely illuminates the lab where now
I'm laid for radiation. Disbelief's
suspended low, gut-shooting me: *pow, pow!*
I'm supine on a slab, in jockey briefs,

belly tattooed down to my hairless groin—
my magic runes, my hexes, blue bullseyes
to burn and burn again till all dots join
across the killing field I visualize

the bad cells dying in (the good, the true
survive their wounds). The great gray Zapper whirrs,
rattles and wheels: vesicles turn to goo,
bowels thin, nerves numb. Deciding faith endures

if one believes it does, I'm naked, spread
taut, as if mounted by my anima,
open to any god's hot thrust, from head
to toenails rigid with desire. Then the

weird vision of a skeleton begins
to form—yes, pumpkin-colored dancing bones—
then broom-borne witches, demons, ghosts, all grins,
and jack-o'-lanterns, R.I.P. tombstones.

Some morbid retinal freak? Some spectral joke?
Can they be celebrating Halloween?
Of course, they're offering up, these gentle folk,
macabre conjure-toons, thumb-tacked between

signs warning DO NOT ENTER—LETHAL ZONE
and DON'T FORGET TO HAVE BLOOD DRAWN.
All read
like glyphs deciphered from Cro-Magnon stone:
"The earth that fed you, now will eat you." *Need*

is shrinking to but one demand: climb down
off this table. The buzzing quits, red eye
clicks out. Modestly in my half-sheet "gown"
I thank the youths who set my dosage high,

and touch hands with the quaking turbaned boy
who's next. Ah, now a host of kids arrives
from Pediatrics. Some can walk. Their joy!—
They're trick-or-treating, costumed in their lives.

The Round

It's a one-round fight because no one
can find the bell to end it and he can't
get to his corner because there is no corner.

The round really *is* round, a blood-stiff
canvas circumference ever-receding. He sways
in the ring's center, and when he gets hit

he staggers back with no ropes to catch him.
Near-blind, he hears above the crowd's boredom
his few fans yelling *My God, stop it!* but never

has there been referee or doctor with such power.
The blow-by-blow announcer keeps shouting
That boy can take tremendous punishment!

And there's no towel or stool or waterbucket
to throw in, no kindly cut-man, no time-out to see
if he's alive. The crowd begins to boo. They

spit and they leave. When he falls he lies
in the debris they threw. But he always gets up,
thinking the only thought left to him—

Just land that last wild devastating punch,
connect with your legendary left hook—just stay
with the fight-plan countless knockdowns can't count out.

So he keeps lurching back in, through bottles
and trash heaped in the ring—the arena silent,
except for the voice rasping in his head—

This time, kid, you're gonna *kill* that sonofabitch.

The Grownup

Now you are the grownup. You look about
for the man who always knows what's done,
but he's dozing through the widow's moan,
half-hidden by a shaky floral cart.

So you're the man to ask. Anyone older
has shrunken to a crone or troll
cackling fear at the oil-stained rail,
sobbing to be unbent off the kneeler.

No longer is it Newark, 1960.
The suit's too tight because you're fat,
not taller, stronger. Drivers await
your instructions. Who of the family

will occupy the rusted limousine?
Widow and daughters ride first, of course;
but next . . . the sons-in-law, or the fierce
aunts, or the uncle whose silver cane

taps out money like you'll never have?
All the wrong choices made, you realize
you've sunk into their ancient ooze
of guilt and envy. It flows like love.

. . .

The vibrant, filthy streets shine
Puerto Rico. To them, it's more disease—

the delis, bakeries, little trattorias
obliterated, gone to shit. You listen,

nod, as if you remember their paradisal
nuova Napoli, Abruzzi, Sicilia;
how endless food, friends, *famiglia*
swirled as one into a thickening circle

unimagined by Dante; all lost, dead.
The limo coughs, smokes; crosses over
the Passaic. (And you think of that doctor
dead upriver, whose gaunt lines fed

on such fumes; wonder how he'd cure
this image-sick moment. *Butt-*
filled silver ashtrays, razor-cut
upholstery . . . anarchy of the poor?)

But the Belleville Diner's still in place.
(Such a brief "cortege": oncoming cars
flash lights: "Hey, idiot, *turn off yours!*")
Cream pies stiffen behind frosted glass.

. . .

It seems you're expected to help carry
the coffin. Suddenly fifty—perhaps it's time
you saw the inside of a mausoleum.
"Priest Available." Any final, sorry

sin, somehow missed till now?—No cost,
today only. Rules prohibit flowers.

New vaults ascend, stacked like file drawers,
and soon a humming hydraulic hoist

will tractor down the marble promenade
and lift a workman seven stories high
to open the "penthouse." "Closer to the sky,
to heaven, and *warmer,*" the salesman said.

You've pulled it off so far. No one sees
you've lost the closest you've come to a father
and, what's stranger still, you even care.
But the visiting anthropologist's pose

must last the day. You learn an elder slips
the priest a twenty, lets him murmur "my son,"
invites him to the funeral feast—yes, *done*
by the gray-haired little boy with aching hips.

Old Drafts

In a hand now strange
over virtual papyrus
wine-blotted (what

was I drinking
through those deep
gone nights?—cheap

half-gallons no doubt
and sweet, thicker so
with alcohol)—

broken-lettered, blotched
with unspeakable encrustations,
who knows what brilliant

riffs and goofs x'd out
when the typewriter
lurched in my eyes like a man

drifting off the shoulder,
swerving back—oh it was all
really very bad stuff and

heaps of it thrown out
in fits of purification,
vain attempted removals

to new lives. Yet these few
saved in a scuffed black
spring binder (of a design

so perfect for young poets
it's no longer made) gave
at their coming into being

crazy joy
better than sex
and good as drugs, abandon

equal to the rock'n'roll
always playing *loud*
at the instant of their creation.

And I was as much then
as now—as even now,
my linguistic prowess peaking—

no, much more then,
the poet, driven
to tears or hilarity

by lines I could not believe
I had made, phrasings
and rhythms accountable

only to the visitations
of wild gods. But truly
very bad it was—

perhaps a small hempen
sack of images
like Sapphic shards

would not now humiliate me,
no more than this
to hold from a writing life

not so cut short as Keats's,
indeed surpassing Shelley's,
which went on and on and did not end

until the thought hit me
Shouldn't I know what I'm doing?
No longer proclaiming

my season as America's
great surrealist, no longer
abject before my master

of the moment, I range
new poems before me
on my immaculately

malleable disc,
every printing perfect,
every copy professional

and impossible
to tell apart
from the original.

Living Will

You know how new lovers bestow
desire on one another and live
long years for its return? Just so,
to you this forgiveness I fore-give,

even certain you'll be half-crazed,
thanking me for it with a curse
the instant you accept it—because
all wrong, this raggedly wrapped verse

crafted to be crushed in your fist,
yours to anneal to iron shadows,
a black slag of sorrow to twist
into some non-form not what it was,

like me. Then, when the hospital's Ethics
Board nods as the chief doctor clicks
and reclicks his pen, miming God
at a loss for the final word

to unmake flesh,
hurl this ruined poem in his face
and say, *Here's his most selfish wish,*
refusing me the plain salt grace

of guilt. And cry *god-damn,* my dearest,
until shocked nurses collapse in prayer.
But then I'll be most blest—my lust
burnt adamant, I'll take my pleasure

with you at last. *Do this:* use force,
but make them free me (you're shriven,
don't forget), while giving me no less
such forgiveness as here fore-given—

which I'll know by this: catch my breath
in your hand passing over my mouth;
then brush your fingers—stroke so smooth!—
down over my eyes; close them both.

Isaac at Sixty

The knife's dull shard of sun
blinds the boy as pain

glimmers in his hips and groin—
a life spent supine,

tensed on a rock-ledge worn
by his weight alone to a form-

fitting altar. The old blade—
mock-ceremonial, blood-

eaten family "carver"—seems
forever suspended by rusty gleams

one cry above the boy's throat,
point dripping drained light

into his eyes. He knows whose hand
holds and withholds it. The man

may be dead muscles, veins,
tendons, balls, bones,

a vast beard of dust, but the stone
bed, on which the boy has lain

for sixty years, still warms
his nerves to spermy scrims

through which he sees
sky smeared with memories

that keep him clenched against
the dead man's strength

to thrust and slash
with the keen corrosion of the past.

Still he waits—the world sweats
its daily fears, as if it cared—awaits

not his lost half-brother's hot
embrace releasing him, but what? . . .

the knife's stab, rending and slow,
when the long-gone grip at last lets go.

Afterword

My first encounter with David Hilton's poetry was in 1970, when I fell hard for his poems in *Quickly Aging Here,* an anthology I brought home from my part-time job at a New Brunswick, New Jersey bookstore. Three years later I ended up going off to college in Madison, Wisconsin, where I renewed my acquaintance with his distinctive work when I came across his first two solo publications—*The Shot Goes In* and *Moving Day*—at that glory-day haven for small-and-even-smaller-press offerings, the Madison Book Co-op. Ever since, I've been a delighted, faithful reader of Hilton's work. I was attracted from the first to the voice that took seriously the very human wonders of the world, all the while refusing to take itself the-wrong-kind-of-seriously; this poet had no time for undue solemnity. His heart was his lodestar, and he was going to do his best to follow it. Whether turning his attention to the stern tract houses of post-wwii San Lorenzo, the more forgiving porches of Madison, Baltimore backyards, the beaches of Mexico, or far-flung European footpaths and byways, Hilton clearly reveled in his peregrinations. Those travels, actual and figurative, are always couched in the language he so judiciously, lovingly tended. A spiritual grandson of Whitman and a son of the good Dr. Williams—with a dash of Uncle Wally Stevens showing up for good measure—this man wrote poems that were plucked from a uniquely Hiltonian garden of down-to-earth verbal delights.

And in 1977, some exquisite serendipity: then-Madison poet and editor Warren Woessner walked up to the table where I was hawking hats and belt-buckles for the Sacred Feather boys on State Street. Although we didn't really know each other very well at the time, Warren invited me to his house for a night of hijinks with this friend of his, Dave Hilton, who was coming from Baltimore for a visit: "I think you guys would really hit it off." I went, eagerly. And amid the drink and smoke and gut-ache laughter, we did indeed hit it off, big time. When Hilton got back home, a more-than-quarter-century of correspondence between us began.

Dave and I spent time together on only three more occasions. In 1985 I went East to give a reading at his college and, of course, to knock around his own colorful version of Baltimore. He came to St. Louis in 1994 and then again in 2001 to celebrate the publication of the final book to appear in his lifetime, *Smoke of My Own Breath* (thirty years after first reading Hilton poems, I had the pleasure of working as his editor on that collection). All told, I spent less than two weeks in his personal company, yet he was one of my closest friends. In our blizzard of correspondence (and I'm talking actual letters, substantial *epistles*—at least a few times a month), we wrote incessantly about books we were reading (and not just "literature," either—he genuinely wanted the details of whatever new flying-saucer tome or nutball-conspiracy treatise I was enthralled by); we wrote about each other's poems, although each of us was oddly shy, forever, about foisting those drafts on the other. Dave recommended films; I recommended *movies*. (On his first visit to St. Louis, Patricia and I took him to see Tim Burton's *Ed Wood,* which he loved. When he admitted that he'd never actually seen any of Maestro Wood's movies themselves, of course I had to mail videos in his direction for months thereafter, insisting that *Plan 9 from Outer Space* was only the tip of the Woodian iceberg. And I'm certain that someday soon Joanne will forgive me, too.) We wrote about whom and what we loved—for Dave, nothing shone brighter than his beloved Joanne and their splendidly nutty life together. A letter from Dave in my mailbox, addressed in his classy script, always meant there were pages in that same hand to pore over later in the day. And maybe, laid in with care, a stray panel clipped out of context from Ernie Bushmiller's surreal-by-accident *Nancy* (my friend had discovered the surest way to appreciate that cartoonist's cockeyed, newspaper-comic-strip vision).

Throughout my poem-reading lifetime, Hilton's poems have always been with me; they have always *mattered*. And with this generous posthumous collection—assembled in the main by the poet himself, even as his sickness continued to wear him down— the world at large gets another shot of the knockout love that's always propelled his finest work. By turns tough and tender, his honest and graceful lines accumulate one more time to sing out their beautiful, eccentric, unabashedly human praises for the work we do, the love we make, and the sheer playing-around we're all better off allowing as much room as possible for. This last dispatch, this *Living Will*, is a legacy that becomes him. Now it belongs to us, too. And because we're all in this together, really, let's make with the joyful noise.

—David Clewell
  St. Louis, September 2006

Colophon

Living Will was designed at Coffee House Press,
in the historic warehouse district of downtown Minneapolis.
The type is set in Spectrum.

Funder Acknowledgment

Coffee House Press is an independent nonprofit literary publisher. Our books are made possible through the generous support of grants and gifts from many foundations, corporate giving programs, individuals, and through state and federal support. This book has received special project support from the Woessner Freeman Foundation. Coffee House Press receives general operating support from the Minnesota State Arts Board, through an appropriation by the Minnesota State Legislature and from the National Endowment for the Arts, a federal agency, and major general operating support from the McKnight Foundation, and from the Target Foundation. Coffee House also receives support from: an anonymous donor; the Elmer and Eleanor Andersen Foundation; the Buuck Family Foundation; the Patrick and Aimee Butler Family Foundation; Gary Fink; Stephen and Isabel Keating; the Lenfesty Family Foundation; Rebecca Rand; the law firm of Schwegman, Lundberg, Woessner & Kluth, P.A.; the James R. Thorpe Foundation; the Archie D. and Bertha H. Walker Foundation; Thompson West; Wood-Rill Foundation; and many other generous individual donors.

This activity is made possible in part by a grant from the Minnesota State Arts Board, through an appropriation by the Minnesota State Legislature and a grant from the National Endowment for the Arts. MINNESOTA STATE ARTS BOARD

 NATIONAL ENDOWMENT FOR THE ARTS

To you and our many readers across the country,
we send our thanks for your continuing support.

Good books are brewing at coffeehousepress.org